A YELLOW Poetry PAINTBOX

Chosen by John Foster

Oxford University Press

Oxford University Press, Walton St, Oxford, OX2 6DP

Oxford   New York
Athens   Auckland   Bangkok   Bombay
Calcutta   Cape Town   Dar es Salaam   Delhi
Florence   Hong Kong   Istanbul   Karachi
Kuala Lumpur   Madras   Madrid   Melbourne
Mexico City   Nairobi   Paris   Singapore
Taipei   Tokyo   Toronto

and associated companies in
Berlin   Ibadan

First published in paperback in 1994
Reprinted 1995

First published in hardback 1994

A CIP catalogue record for this book is available
from the British Library.

Illustrations by

Renée Andriani, Jane Bottomley, Bucket, Caroline Crossland,
Paul Dowling, Fiona Dunbar, Yajia Gao, David Holmes,
Rhian Nest James, Jan Lewis, Graham Round, Jessica Thomson, Jenny Williams.

ISBN 0 19 916677 3 (paperback)
ISBN 0 19 916718 4 (hardback)

Printed in Hong Kong

Contents

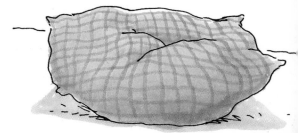

Guess who?

Who chews a hole
   in the kitchen door?
Who makes puddles
   on the floor?

4

Who wags her tail
and chases the cat?
Who eats Dad's slippers
and rips up the mat?

Who tries to jump
the garden gate?
Who steals my dinner
from my plate?

Who runs to meet me
    every day?
Who rolls on her back
    when she wants to play?

Who's my best friend?
   Well, can't you guess?
My best friend is
   my puppy Jess.

Marie Brookes

In my garden

In my garden,
My pets are free.
Sometimes they come
To play with me—
Butterflies, all kinds of bugs,
Ladybirds and snails and slugs,
Caterpillars and bumble-bees
Which live among the grass and
trees.

Gwenda Izzet

My goldfish

My goldfish is
   the perfect pet.
She isn't any trouble.
She doesn't bark.
She doesn't mew,
   just bubbles
       bubbles
       bubbles.

My goldfish is
　　the perfect pet.
She isn't any trouble.
We don't have
　　to feed her much.
She doesn't need
　　a rabbit hutch,
　　　just bubbles
　　　　　bubbles
　　　　　　bubbles.

Marie Brookes

Pet talk

Jamie has a cat,
Jimmy has a dog;
Jennie has a gerbil,
Jilly has a frog.

Mandy has a budgie,
Michael has a horse;
Maggie has a rabbit
and *I* have...

      a BABY BROTHER,
           of course!

Judith Nicholls

Bonfire Night

In the night-time darkness,
In the night-time cold,
Did you spot a catherine wheel
Raining showers of gold?
Did you watch a rocket
Go zoom into the sky?
And hear a bonfire crackle
As the sparks lit up the guy?
In the night-time darkness,
In the night-time cold,
Did you clutch a sparkler
As it scattered stars of gold?

Irene Yates

Chinese New Year

Dragons, lions,
Red and gold.
In with the New Year,
Out with the old.

Banners flying,
Bands playing.
Lion prancing,
Dragon swaying.

16

Fireworks cracking,
Lanterns swinging,
People laughing,
Dancing, singing.

Dragons, lions,
Red and gold.
In with the New Year,
Out with the Old.

Wendy Larmont

Eid-Mubarak

There's Granny, Uncle, Aunty,
my cousins at the back.
They're hugging Mum and Daddy.
We cry, 'Eid-Mubarak.'
We've had lots of cards
and presents,
there's a knocking at the door.
Can it be my Grandad
bringing us some more?
Yes, it's really Grandad.
What's that behind his back?
We hug him in the hallway
and shout, 'Eid-Mubarak.'

Marian Swinger

Christmas Eve

Nearly midnight;
still can't sleep!
Has he been yet?
Dare I peep?

Sneak out softly,
creaking floor!
Down the stairs
and through the door . . .
In the darkness
by the tree,
tightly wrapped . . .
but which for me?

Feel the ribbon,
find the card!
This one? That one?
Heart thumps hard.
Trembling fingers,
throbbing head,
then . . .

a voice yells

'BACK TO BED!'

Judith Nicholls

At Bimla's house last night

At Bimla's house last night
We had fireworks and
Sparklers and rice and
Sweet, juicy
Jum-jums bigger than
Gobstoppers.

At Bimla's house last night
Her Dad lit up
All the rooms with candles
And down in the kitchen
Her Mum was so pleased
She gave me a hug.
At Bimla's house last night
We all sang
Songs and wished each other

Happy Divali!

Irene Yates

Adventure at breakfast time

Here comes Batman
Zooming across our garden
To save the cat from
The dinosaur
That lives next door.

And here comes She-ra
Zapping along the front path
To check the milk bottles
For bat-juice, dragonfly-wings
And other
Very nasty things.

And here comes Egon
Zooming through the kitchen door
To rescue the dog from
The ghost
That slurps the butter
Off my toast.

And here comes our Dad
Zapping down the stairs
To give them all a
Telling off
And send them away
Because
I can't go out to play
Till I've finished
My breakfast.

Irene Yates

Pirates

Let's play pirates.
Let's pretend.
This chair's a ship:
the front's my end.

Yes, great!

I'm the captain.
You're the crew,
so I can tell you
what to do.

Yes, great!

OK then, you're
a lower rank,
so now you've got
to walk the plank.

Yes, grea

a

a

a

r

g

h

h

h

!

Charles Thomson

Pretending

I sit on the swing and I fly up high.
I am a brave spaceman
    exploring the sky.

I stand on my bed and I jump
   up and down.
I tumble and fall. I'm a circus clown.

I sit in my bath and I play with my ship.
There are rocks and sharks.
   It's a dangerous trip.

I lie in my bed and I close my eyes tight.
My bed is a ship which I sail
    through the night.

John Foster

Sometimes I pretend

Sometimes I pretend
I am a giant,
With feet so HUGE
I squash the houses
In our street
Each time I move!

Sometimes I pretend
I am an ant,
With feet so small
I tiptoe by
And no one knows
I'm there at all!

Trevor Harvey

When Susie's eating custard

When Susie's eating custard,
It splashes everywhere—
Down her bib, up her nose,
All over her high chair.

She pokes it with her fingers.
She spreads it on her hair.
When Susie's eating custard,
She gets it everywhere.

John Foster

When the giant comes to breakfast

When the giant comes to breakfast
He eats Corn Flakes with a spade,
Followed by a lorry load
Of toast and marmalade.
Next, he takes a dustbin
Fills it up with tea,
Drinks it all in a gulp,
And leaves the mess for me.

John Coldwell

39

Picnic tea

We found a shady spot under a tree.
Here's what we had for a picnic tea.

We had ants in the sandwiches,
      wasps in the jam,
      slugs in the lettuce leaves,
      beetles in the ham,
      midges in the orange juice,
      flies on the cheese,
      spiders on the sausages,
      ice-cream full of bees!

David Harmer

Did you really?

Dip, dip, dip!
Did you ever lick
a lollipop stick
dipped into the mustard?
Did it make you sick?

My, my, my!
Did you ever try
a popcorn pie
chopped up with an onion?
Did it make you cry?

Hoo, hoo, hoo!
Did you ever chew
a bubble-gum stew
mixed up with some custard?
Can I have some too?

Judith Nicholls

Time for...?

Christopher Sweet tucked his feet
down to the bottom
of the warm, warm sheet.
*How many times
did the Church clock strike?
One, two, three, four, five,
six, seven, EIGHT!*

Caroline Tate is always late,
she's only just running
through the old school gate!
*How many times
did the school bell chime?*
*One, two, three, four, five,
six, seven, eight, NINE!*

Oliver Lee can't wait for tea,
school's nearly finished for him and me!
How many rings till we're all free?
One, two, THREE!

Nicola Head won't go to bed.
'Chase her up the stairs then'
her mother said.
How many times
did the clock strike then?
One, two, three, four, five,
six, seven, eight, nine, TEN!

Marilyn Heap is fast asleep;
listen at the door
but you won't hear a peep!
How many times
did the Church clock strike?
One, two, three, four, five,
six, seven, eight, nine, ten,
eleven, twelve . . . MIDNIGHT!

Judith Nicholls

The lost sock

I've lost one of my socks.
It's yellow and blue.
Now I've only one sock.
This morning I'd two.

I've lost one of my socks.
I've looked everywhere.
This morning I'd two—
And two make a pair.

I've lost one of my socks.
What shall I do?
How did it get there?
It's inside my shoe!

Marie Brookes

Shoes

Red shoes, blue shoes,
Old shoes, new shoes,
Shoes that are black,
Shoes that are white,
Shoes that are loose,
Shoes that are tight.
Shoes with buckles,
Shoes with bows,
Shoes that are narrow
And pinch your toes.

Shoes that are yellow,
Shoes that are green,
Shoes that are dirty,
Shoes that are clean.
Shoes for cold weather,
Shoes for when it's hot.
Shoes with laces
That get tangled in a knot!

John Foster

There's a hole in my pants

There's a hole in my pants.
It's our washing machine.
It's eating our clothes,
Not washing them clean.

As it churns round and round,
It snorts and it snickers,
Chewing holes in Dad's shirts
And ripping Mum's knickers.

It's swallowed a sock.
We can't open the door.
It's bubbling out soap suds
All over the floor.

There's a monster that lives
In our washing machine.
It's eating our clothes,
Not washing them clean.

John Foster

Princess Kirandip

At school in the week
I wear
A grey skirt and
Green jumper, just like my best friend
And we pretend we're twins.
But on Saturdays and Sundays
I wear my
Shiny, shiny blue
Kameeze and langa
With a tuni to cover my head,
All covered with silver stars—
And Tracey
Stares at me and says
'Oh, Kirandip—
You must be a princess!'

And I feel good.

Irene Yates

My clean blouse

Look at my blouse!
It was clean today.
I tried very hard
To keep it that way.

Do you like my painting?
It's a bird in the sky.
But I leaned on the paper
Before it was dry.

Then at play time I joined in
A great game of chase
But I tripped on a stone
And fell flat on my face.

At lunch time, somebody,
Peter, I think,
Bumped into me just as I
Picked up my drink.

Then on the way home
I was splashed by a lorry.
I tried to stay clean, Mum.
Believe me. I'm sorry.

John Coldwell

Index of first lines

Acknowledgements

The Editor and Publisher are grateful for permission to include the following poems:

Marie Brookes for 'The lost sock', 'Guess who?' and 'My goldfish' all © 1991 Marie Brookes; John Coldwell for 'My clean blouse' © 1991 John Coldwell; John Foster for 'Pretending', 'Shoes', 'There's a hole in my pants' and 'When Susie's eating custard' all © 1991 John Foster; David Harmer for 'Picnic tea' © 1991 David Harmer; Trevor Harvey for 'Sometimes I pretend' © 1991 Trevor Harvey; Gwenda Izzet for 'In my garden' © 1991 Gwenda Izzet; Wendy Larmont for 'Chinese New Year' © 1991 Wendy Larmont; Judith Nicholls for 'Christmas Eve', 'Did you really?', 'Pet talk' and 'Time for . . . ?' all © 1991 Judith Nicholls; Marian Swinger for 'Eid-Mubarak' © 1991 Marian Swinger; Charles Thomson for 'Pirates' © 1991 Charles Thomson; Irene Yates for 'Adventure at breakfast time', 'Bonfire night', 'At Bimla's house last night' and 'Princess Kirandip' all © 1991 Irene Yates.